GETTING WELL

A Study for Children About Spiritual and Physical Healing

John I. Penn

Reproducible

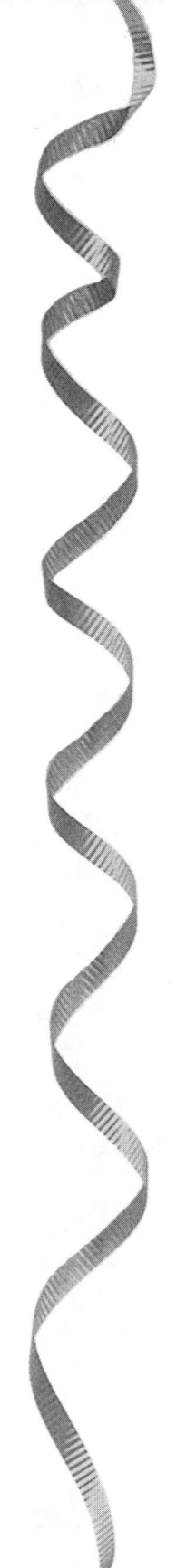

Getting Well

A Study for Children About
Spiritual and Physical Healing

by John I. Penn

Designer and Illustrator: Paige Easter
Editors: Peg Augustine and Judy Newman-St. John
Associate Editor: Alex Petrounov
Production Editor: David Whitworth

Unless otherwise noted, Scripture quotations are from
the New Revised Standard Version of the Bible,
copyright 1989, Division of Christian Education of the National Council
of the Churches of Christ in the United States of America. Used by permission. All rights reserved.

Scripture quotations marked (CEV) are from the Contemporary English Version
Copyright © 1991, 1992, 1995 by American Bible Society, Used by permission.

Illustration Credits: Page 9: Brenda Gilliam. © 2008 Cokesbury. Page 20: Robert S. Jones.
© 1998 Abingdon Press. Page 59: Robert S. Jones. © 2001 Abingdon Press.
All other illustrations by Paige Easter. © 2008 Abingdon Press.

ISBN 978-0-687-00720-2

08 09 10 11 12 13 14 15 16 17—10 9 8 7 6 5 4 3 2 1

Manufactured in the United States of America.

DEDICATION

This book, *Getting Well*, is dedicated to a very special and courageous little girl, Shidah Aiken. She taught us so much about life and living to the fullest, while suffering with leukemia. She taught us how to love even the unlovable, because this is what God expects of us all.

Shidah, you will always live in our hearts and memory.

*Loving God, thank you for touching our lives through
the gift of Shidah, even for such a short time!
The prophet Isaiah said, "And a little child shall lead them"
(Isaiah 11:6).*

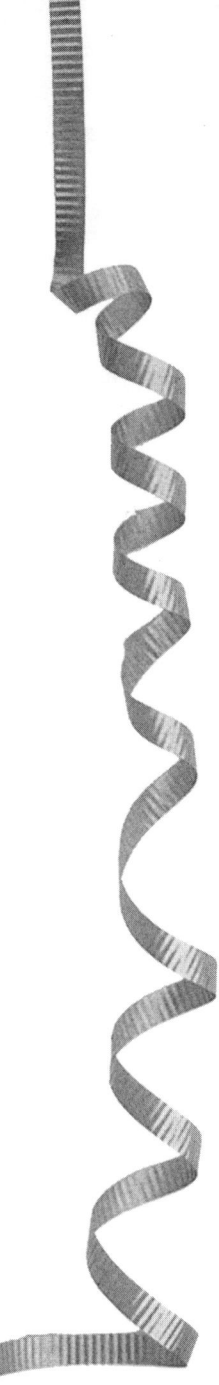

Table of Contents

Introduction

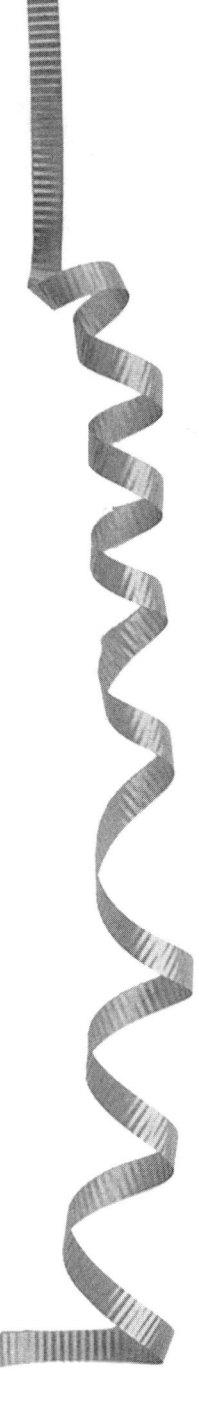

Welcome! The next six weeks can be an exciting time for you as you help your group explore healing and wholeness. Today's nine-to-twelve year-olds, popularly known as "tweens," are well versed in pop culture. They are in the know concerning the latest clothing fashions, the hottest songs, the best video games, the most popular athletes, and the coolest Hollywood idols. They can sing word-for-word the newest and catchiest commercial jingles. Most are computer literate and well versed in the latest electronic technology. They have seen many hours of television programming on hospitals and life-and-death issues. They may have even seen programs on miraculous healing. And they have questions they may not even be able to articulate.

The Bible is a good place to learn about the importance of healing and its place in the Christian church. Not only did Jesus heal people, he also taught his disciples to heal as he had done. In fact, Jesus made it clear that healing was a sign of the coming kingdom of God (Matthew 10:1, 7-8). His followers were to continue his threefold ministry of teaching, preaching, and healing both in their community and in the world.

We know too that healing was an expectation of the early church. The Epistle of James affirms that healing was a vital ministry. The church was endowed with the gifts of the Holy Spirit for the common good, including healing (1 Corinthians 12:9).

We live in a broken world in need of healing. The church is God's healing agent in the world. As followers of Jesus we are called to spread the good news that God wants everyone to be a whole person in every dimension of life: spirit, body, mind (emotions), and relationships. The selected healing stories and the activities included in this study tell about the depth of God's love.

Your children will learn
- what healing is
- why Jesus healed
- what healing teaches us about God's love for us
- why healing is needed today
- how to enhance health in every stage of life by choosing lifestyles that promote wholeness.

Before You Begin

- ☐ Read through the study.

- ☐ Pray for yourself and your group.

- ☐ Photocopy the activity sheets for each student.

- ☐ Provide a folder with brackets and lined paper for journaling for each child.

- ☐ Provide a paper punch for the children to use to add their activity sheets and other photocopies to the folder.

- ☐ Gather pens, pencils, and markers.

- ☐ Have several copies of *The Contemporary English Version of the Bible* for the students to use. You may want to have a copy of *The Message* as well.

- ☐ The following books are recommended for additional reading. Some of them may be found in your church library.

Anna, Jesus Loves You by James K. Wagner. Upper Room Books, 1985.
ISBN-13: 978-0835805124.

The Wing by Ray Buckley. Abingdon Press, 2002. ISBN-13: 978-0687097043.

Christmas Moccasins by Ray Buckley. Abingdon Press, 2003.
ISBN-13: 978-0687027385.

We Are All the Same: A Story of a Boy's Courage and a Mother's Love by Jim Wooten.
Penguin Press, 2005. ISBN-13: 978-0143035992.

A Coloring and Activities Book

• To complement your study

About Caring and Healing: A Coloring and Activities Book
by John I. Penn.
Illustrations by Wanda Parker Rains.
$5.00 per copy

Copies may be ordered from
John I. Penn
parkerpenn@verizon.net

Fearfully and Wonderfully Made

Main Idea

God created each one of us perfectly and loves us as we are.

Scripture

I praise you because of the wonderful way you created me. Everything you do is marvelous!
Psalm 139:14, CEV

Key Words

Abnormality • a condition that is not normal

Cure • a method of restoring health

Disease • anything that diminishes health in an organ or body part

Heal • to make well

Incurable • a health condition that cannot be corrected

Unclean • dirty or impure

Wholeness • wellness

Get Ready

- Gather all the supplies you will need for this session.
- Mark Psalm 139:13-16, John 5:3-17, and Luke 5:12-16 in your Bible.
- Read the information about Jeff Steinberg (*Activity Sheet 3*) so you can share it with the class.
- Write the Key Words on newsprint.
- On another sheet of newsprint write the Bible memory verse for today: Psalm 139:14.
- On still another sheet write: "I am a miracle! I am God's special creation! I was made from love by a loving God."
- Write each word of Psalm 139:14 (CEV) on a separate index card.
- Write the words *body, mind, spirit,* and *relationships* across the top of a sheet of newsprint. Draw lines to divide the newsprint into four columns under those headings.
- Cut white paper into 8½-inch squares.

BIBLE BACKGROUND
Psalm 139:13-16
John 5:3-17
Luke 5:12-16

SUPPLIES
CEV Bibles
student journals (see p. 6)
photocopies of Activity Sheets 1-5 (pp. 35-39)
3-hole paper punch
newsprint or large pieces of paper
white paper
colored construction paper
scissors
markers, pens, pencils
gluesticks
masking tape
safety pins
large index cards

Welcome

- Welcome the students warmly.

- If this is not your regular class, ask the students to make nametags (*Activity Sheet 1*). Encourage them to write their names. Suggest they use their birthdate as the RX number (for example, July 28, 1998, would be 7281998). Show the students how to put a loop of masking tape through a safety pin to pin their nametags to their clothes.

- Have the folders with brackets and lined paper ready for each student to begin a journal.

SAY: *We are going to begin learning together about healing and wholeness. We will learn about God's unlimited love for us and God's desire for us to be healthy and whole in every area of our lives—spirit, body, mind (emotions), and relationships. Each week we will learn some Key Words that will help guide our study.*

- Ask the students to copy the Key Words for this session and their definitions in their journals. Ask if anyone has heard any of the words used and what the circumstances were when they heard the words.

Word Search Fun

- Ask for volunteers to read Psalm 139:13-16 from the CEV and perhaps also from *The Message*.

SAY: *Here King David describes how God made and shaped him as a unique creation. He knew that every human being is an amazing creation. That includes you! When everything in our lives and in our bodies is working as it should, we say we are "whole." A very important part of being a whole person, though, is to accept who we are. For some people that is not as easy as it sounds. Some of us have a hard time accepting ourselves as we are—as God created us. Some people think they are too tall or too short, too fat or too skinny, too smart or too dumb, and so on.*

ASK: *What is one thing you really like about yourself? (Accept answers.) What is one thing you would like to change about yourself? (Accept answers.)*

CONTINUE: *But being a whole person does not mean being perfect. Everyone is created by God to be just that person—wonderful and unique. That includes even those persons who look different because they were born without some of their body parts or who were born with some sort of abnormality.*

- Give each student a copy of the word search (*Activity Sheet 2*). Invite everyone to find the words from Psalm 139:13-16. Let the students punch holes in their pages and add them to their journals.

Paper Snowflakes

- Give each student an 8½-inch square of paper.

- Show everyone step-by-step how to fold the paper. Fold the square paper in half to create a big triangle.

- Fold that triangle in half to make a smaller triangle.

- Hold the triangle with the longest side at the top. This is Side C. Mark a spot about three inches from the right edge on Side C.

- Fold Side A over until it touches that spot on Side C.
- Fold Side B over Side A as shown.
- Cut off the two points that are sticking up as shown.
- The tallest point of the triangle will be the center of the snowflake. Use scissors to cut a few small swirls and spikes. Leave at least some of the folded edge intact so the snowflake doesn't fall apart. Open the paper to see the ornate snowflake.

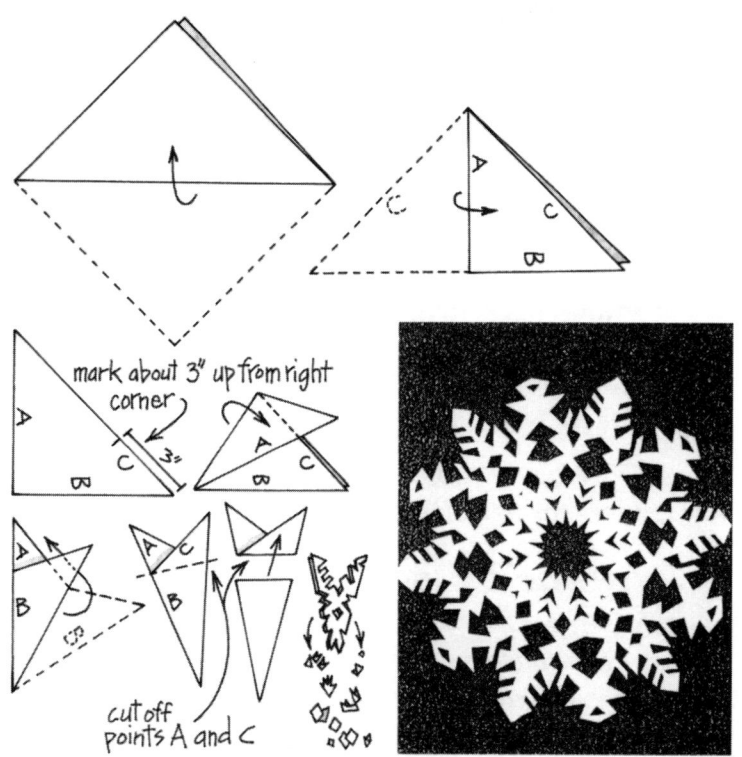

mark about 3" up from right corner

cut off points A and C

SAY: *Each of your snowflakes is unique, one-of-a-kind. God created each of us to be unique and one-of-a-kind.*

- Let each student select a color of construction paper and marker. Have them use gluesticks to glue their snowflakes to the paper to create a poster.
- Point out the newsprint with the words "I am a miracle." Invite the students to add any or all of the phrases to their snowflake posters.

Jeff Steinberg

- Pass out the information about Jeff Steinberg *(Activity Sheet 3)*.
- Ask for a volunteer to read the story.
- Ask the students to punch holes and add the sheet to their journals.

SAY: *Jeff is a whole person in the truest sense. Jeff is a dynamic Christian and a gifted professional singer. His song "I Am a Masterpiece in Process" celebrates who he is and whose he is. He is a whole person who happens to have a body that is different from most other people's bodies. Like each snowflake, Jeff has a one-of-a-kind body. So do you. Jeff gives thanks for his creation. He loves God and he also loves himself. He knows that no matter how we look we are made in the image of God. Jeff gives thanks and celebrates the body that God gave him, because he knows and feels loved and affirmed by his Creator. When you accept and love yourself the way God does, you will be fully alive and fully whole and fully appreciate your uniqueness. His outward appearance does not make him wonderful. What makes every person a wonder is that he or she is made in the image of God!*

- If the students want to learn more about Jeff, have them look at *www.tinygiant.com*.

The Bible Teaches Us

SAY: *Jesus knew that to be fully alive and fully whole, we must live lives of love. That means loving God, our neighbors, and ourselves. Today we will hear about two men Jesus healed. These stories tell us some important truths about God's love.*

- Ask a volunteer to read John 5:3-17.

- Ask "I wonder" questions. ("I wonder" questions give students a chance to voice opinions in a safe way.) I wonder

  —why Jesus wanted to heal this man.

  —why Jesus asked the man if he wanted to be made whole.

  —why the man responded to Jesus as he did.

ASK: *When did the man's healing come? What reason did Jesus give to the religious leaders for healing the man? What does this reveal about God?*

True or False?

SAY: *Another story tells us about Jesus' encounter with a person who had leprosy. Leprosy was considered highly infectious. People who had it were "unclean" and they could not live with people who did not have the disease. When they saw other people approaching, they had to cry out, "Unclean, unclean," so that the others could avoid them. They could not work. They had to depend on the help and mercy of their families for their needs of food, water, and upkeep. Often they were neglected and left to beg for food and resources they needed to live day by day.*

- Ask a volunteer to read Luke 5:12-16.

- Give each student a photocopy of the true/false questions (*Activity Sheet 4*).

SAY: *You may work in pairs to answer the true or false questions.*

- Call everyone back together to discuss the questions and answers.

- Invite the students to add their pages to their journals.

SAY: *Jesus shows us what God's love for us is like. Even though the leper was considered unclean and unlovable, Jesus cared for him and healed him. God loves each of us just as we are. God created each one of us to be wonderful, and God loves us.*

Write God's Word on Your Heart

- Point out the newsprint where you wrote today's Bible memory verse (Psalm 139:14).

- Ask everyone to read the verse together two times. Remove the newsprint. (Keep the newsprint copy of the Bible verse to use again next week.)

- Display the index cards with the words of the verse placed in the correct order. Have everyone say the verse again. Randomly remove four or five cards and let the students guess the missing words. Repeat again, but remove different words. Continue until the students can say the verse with most of the cards missing.

- Give each student a copy of the Bible verse (*Activity Sheet 5*) to decorate and add to their journals.

Spiritual Workout

- Display the newsprint with the words *body*, *mind*, *spirit*, and *relationships*.

SAY: *Being a whole person involves our bodies, our minds, our spirits, and our relationships with others. That is what makes us healthy. What are some things you can do regularly to have a healthy lifestyle?* (*Accept answers. Help them think of eating healthy food, drinking plenty of water, getting enough sleep, exercising, reading books, listening to music, reading the Bible, praying, and helping others. Write each one on the newsprint under the correct heading. Make a plus sign [+] by each one.*) **What are some things that we can do that keep us from being healthy in these four areas?** (*Accept answers. Help them think of eating unhealthy foods, drinking, smoking, taking drugs, lying, cheating, having bad attitudes, and being unkind to others. Write each one on the newsprint under the correct heading. Make a minus sign [–] by each one.*)

CONTINUE: *Make a chart like this in your journal. List both the good* (*positive*) ***and bad*** (*negative*) ***things you do in all of these areas. Be honest—this list is just for you. No one else will see it. Then write a plan of what you can do to make your lifestyle more healthy. Make it simple and something you can actually complete. Each night before you go to bed check to see how well you have done during the day. If you wish, ask your family for help.***

- If time allows, let the students begin their charts in their journals. Encourage them to think carefully and reflect on what it means to them personally.

Suggested Books

Have these suggested books for the students to read. You might let the students borrow the books to read at home and return them next week.

Anna, Jesus Loves You by James K. Wagner (Upper Room Books, 1985).

The Wing by Ray Buckley (Abingdon Press, 2002).

If time permits, read *The Wing* aloud. Point out that even though the bird "She Who Flies Swiftly" was not healed physically, she was made whole.

Close With Prayer

- Ask for prayer requests. Write them on a sheet of newsprint. Then pray, thanking God for the class, for stories in the Bible that help us grow, and for God's love in Jesus. Pray for each prayer request.

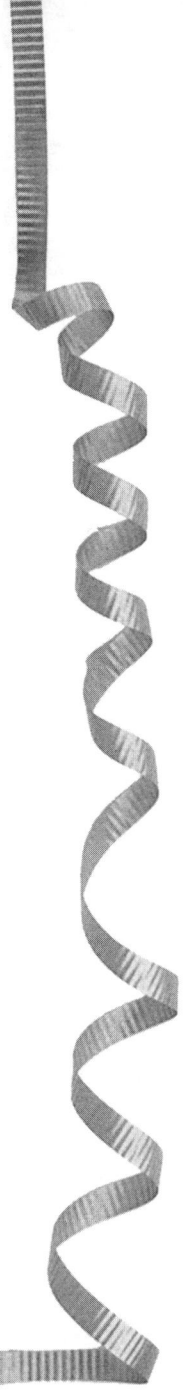

God's Love Makes Us Whole

BIBLE BACKGROUND
1 John 4:10-11
Ephesians 1:1-5
Psalm 139:14
Luke 15:11-32

Main Idea

No one is beyond God's love.

Scripture

Real love isn't our love for God, but his love for us. God sent his Son to be the sacrifice by which our sins are forgiven. Dear friends, since God loved us this much, we must love each other. 1 John 4:10-11, CEV

Key Words

Church • a community of believers in Christ

Conversion • change of heart

Grace • undeserved love and mercy of God

Salvation • the act of being saved or rescued

Shalom • God's perfect peace

Get Ready

- Gather all the supplies you will need for this session.
- Mark 1 John 4:10-11, Ephesians 1:1-5, Psalm 139:14, and Luke 15:11-32 in your Bible.
- Write the Key Words on a sheet of newsprint.
- On a large posterboard write the words "No one is beyond God's love."
- On a sheet of newsprint write the memory verse for today: 1 John 4:10-11.
- Photocopy the Bible verse strips *(Activity Sheet 8)*, cut them apart, and place them in an envelope. Your group will be divided into teams of three or four. You will need a set of Bible verse strips for each team.

SUPPLIES
CEV Bibles
student journals (see p. 6)
photocopies of Activity Sheets 6-11 (pp. 40-45)
3-hole paper punch
nametags from Session 1
newsprint from Session 1 with Psalm 139:14
newsprint or large pieces of paper
posterboard
magazines
scissors
glue
diluted glue mixture
(about 3 parts water to 1 part glue)
old brushes
markers, pens, pencils
envelopes

Welcome

- Welcome the students warmly.

- Ask the students to wear the nametags they made during the first session.

- Ask the students to copy the Key Words for this session and their definitions in their journals. Ask if anyone has heard any of the words used and what the circumstances were when they heard the words.

SAY: *Last week we talked about what it means to be a whole person in our body, mind, spirit, and relationships. We also began to think about some of the things we sometimes do that keep us from being healthy and whole in those areas. Those things make us feel like we are broken. We thought about how living a life of love makes us whole. It is very true that no one is beyond God's love. Even when we are feeling out-of-sorts and wondering if anyone does love us, God's love is there. God loved us before we were born and God will never stop loving us.*

No One Is Beyond God's Love

- Place the posterboard with the words "No one is beyond God's love" on the table.

- Invite the students to search through old magazines for pictures of people's faces. Have them cut or tear out the pictures and glue them to the newsprint. Encourage them to let the pictures touch or overlap so the paper is filled.

SAY: *Each person in these pictures is different. Each person has joys and problems, strengths and difficulties. No matter what, no person is beyond God's love. God's love makes each of us whole.*

- If the materials on the collage do not stick perfectly after gluing, let the students use old brushes to brush a diluted glue mixture (about 3 parts water to 1 part glue) over the whole collage. This will also seal the collage and make it glossy.

The Bible Teaches Us

- Invite a volunteer to read Ephesians 1:1-5.

ASK: *Did Paul always love Jesus and share God's love with others?* (*If the students do not know or remember about Paul, explain that Paul hated Christians and persecuted them until his experience on the Damascus Road. From that time on, he spent his life devoted to God.*)

SAY: *Paul had a conversion experience and he changed. He was amazed when he realized that God loved him after all the bad things he had done. He spent his life telling others that no matter how badly we have messed up, God still loves us. Everyone is a creation of God's love. No one is beyond God's love.*

- Point out the newsprint with last week's memory verse. Invite everyone to say the verse with you: "I praise you because of the wonderful way you created me. Everything you do is marvelous!" (Psalm 139:14, CEV).

SAY: *When people don't know that they are loved they lose hope, and they don't live up to what they could be—they don't live up to their true potential. God sent Jesus to help us know about God's love and to know God's purpose for our lives.*

CONTINUE: *Jesus made God's plan so simple—love God and love others. Love should be a way of life for all. Jesus came to show us how to love God's way. When*

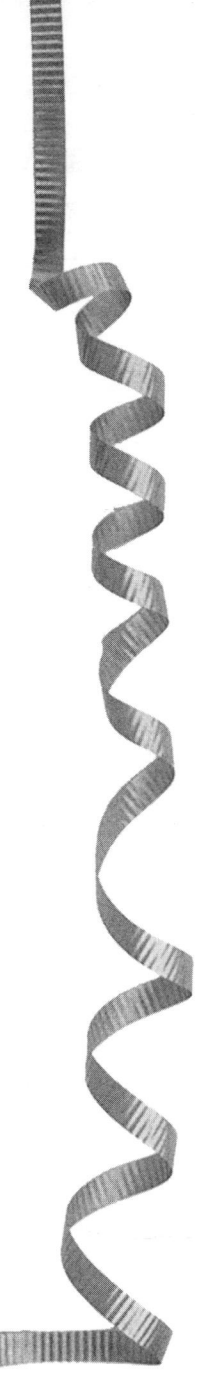

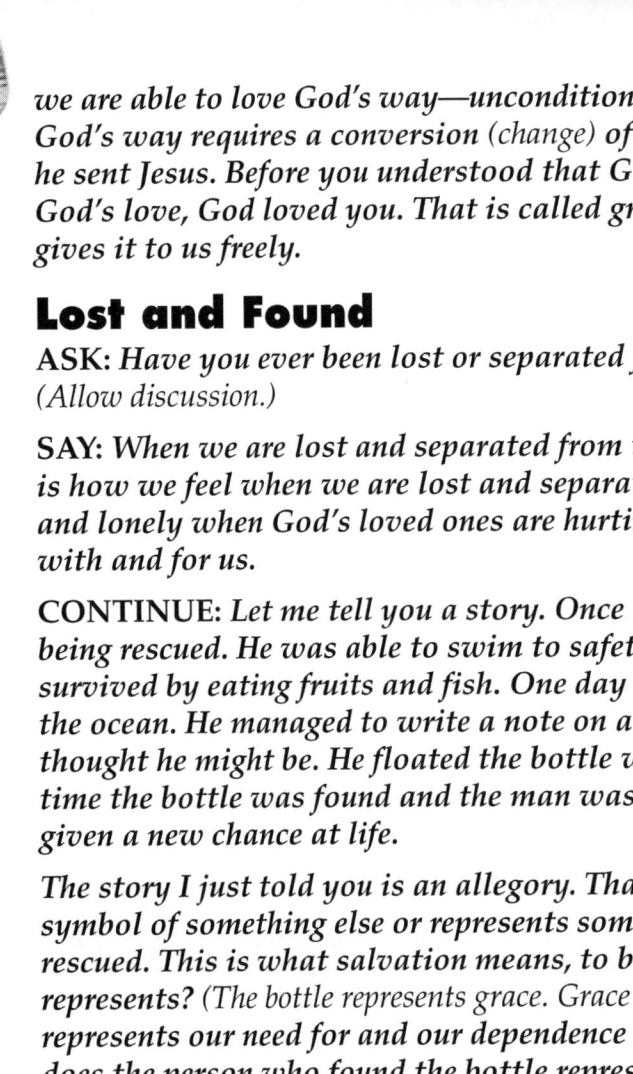

we are able to love God's way—unconditionally—it is like being born again. Loving God's way requires a conversion (change) of the heart. God had you in mind when he sent Jesus. Before you understood that God loves you or could even respond to God's love, God loved you. That is called grace. We don't deserve it or earn it; God gives it to us freely.

Lost and Found

ASK: *Have you ever been lost or separated from your family? How did you feel? (Allow discussion.)*

SAY: *When we are lost and separated from those who love us, we are afraid. This is how we feel when we are lost and separated from God's love. God also feels sad and lonely when God's loved ones are hurting and afraid. God grieves and suffers with and for us.*

CONTINUE: *Let me tell you a story. Once a man was lost at sea with no hope of being rescued. He was able to swim to safety to the nearest island beach. He survived by eating fruits and fish. One day he found a bottle with a cap floating in the ocean. He managed to write a note on a piece of his undershirt telling where he thought he might be. He floated the bottle with the note out to sea. After a long time the bottle was found and the man was rescued. In a very real sense he was given a new chance at life.*

The story I just told you is an allegory. That means each part of the story is a symbol of something else or represents something else. The story is of a man being rescued. This is what salvation means, to be rescued. What do you think the bottle represents? (The bottle represents grace. Grace is God's love and mercy for us.) The note represents our need for and our dependence on the one who comes to save us. Who does the person who found the bottle represent? (Jesus. Jesus came to bring God's Shalom to the world. Shalom means peace, but much more. It is a word that describes the wholeness of life that God wants for God's people.)

ASK: *Does anyone remember the question Jesus asked the man who was healed in last week's story? ("Do you want to be healed?") Our biggest problem is not the brokenness that comes from outside of ourselves but the brokenness that comes from inside. We have to answer that question too. Do we want to be made whole?*

SAY: *When we come to know God's love, we want to do the things God wants us to do. One of the things God wants us to do is to take care of our bodies. Sometimes when we just aren't feeling right it may be because we have eaten a lot of junk food or stayed up late or not gotten any exercise, or we may not be at peace with others. There are really simple things we can do to make ourselves feel better. Look at the list on **Activity Sheet 6** and write your sentences. Be honest. No one will see it but you. Over the next week take a look at it each day and see if you can improve on any of your choices.*

The Prodigal Son

SAY: *One of the great lost-and-found stories is the story of the prodigal son.*

- Invite a volunteer to read Luke 15:11-32.

- Let the students play a game to enjoy the story. Have one volunteer be blindfolded and play the Father. Have another student play the Son. Ask everyone else to be the Pigs.

SAY: *After the son left home, he became so poor and so hungry that he took care of pigs. That was quite a change from the life he had been used to. When he returned home, his father was overjoyed, forgave him, and welcomed him home. To play this game, everyone spread out and walk around slowly. Keep moving. The Son should call out, "I'm sorry, Father. Please let me come home." The Father should call out, "Son, you are forgiven. Welcome home." While they are calling out, all the Pigs should oink as loud as they can. Let's see if the Father can find his Son.*

- Let the students play. Watch carefully to be sure the blindfolded child plays safely. If they wish, have two other volunteers become the Father and Son and play the game again.

ASK: *When does God forgive us? (Whenever we ask and sincerely want to change.) Who will God forgive? (All people.) Why? (No one is beyond God's love.)*

Put Love Into Action

SAY: *Just like the father in this parable, God's love is always there waiting for us. But it is not enough just to accept that love. When we decide to become followers of Jesus, one of the things we will want to do is to tell others about God's love. Sometimes we say we need to put love into action. That means that we have to show people God's love by loving them.*

ASK: *How can we do that? (Guide the discussion, suggesting that we need to start where we are. We can try to love everyone, not just those like us. Help them think of concrete examples of loving actions. Make a list on newsprint as you continue this discussion.)*

SAY: *One of the best ways of putting love into action is to accept people for what they are. Jesus encouraged his followers to reach out to everyone to bring the broken ones back. That is why it was important to Jesus to touch the leper in the story last week. To others of the day a leper was a throwaway person. Jesus' touch said to the man, "You are a child of God." Jesus' touch was just as important as his words.*

CONTINUE: *Just as the father forgave his son in today's story, we can help others find God's love through forgiveness. You can teach others to forgive by your action of forgiving others. Forgiveness brings wholeness and healing to both persons—the one who did the wounding and the one who was wounded. Both are healed and made whole.*

CONTINUE: *Jesus calls us to be healers—to lift up the poor, clothe those without clothes, give shelter to the homeless, and visit the lonely. By ourselves we may not be able to make huge changes in the world, but we can be creative and find ways to reach out to others. Everything we do will make a difference.*

ASK: *What are some things we can do as a class? (Accept answers. Make a list on newsprint. Add any of the following to the list that were not thought of by the students: We can visit in nursing homes and sing or do skits for the people there. We can collect cards and small gifts like socks and T-shirts for people who are in prison. We can adopt a family who has just moved into our community—we can introduce ourselves to them and show them around our community and help them find their classrooms at school.)*

- Talk about each suggestion on the list. What supplies would be needed? How much time would be needed? When could we do this project? Who else would need to be involved? Based on the circumstances of your group, help them choose the project that best fits their ability.

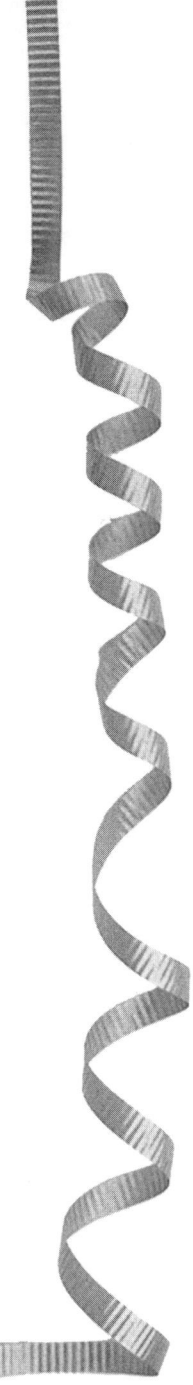

Make and Send

- Give each student a photocopy of *Activity Sheet 7*.
- Set out scissors, markers, pens, and other supplies you have on hand.
- Invite the children to decorate the cards for the people on your church's prayer list.
- Provide envelopes for the cards and see that they are mailed.

Write God's Word on Your Heart

- Divide the students into teams of three or four depending on the size of your group.
- Give each team an envelope containing the Bible verse strips *(Activity Sheet 8)*.
- Display the newsprint on which you have written today's Bible verse. Ask everyone to read the verse with you three times. Remove the newsprint.
- Explain that you will give the teams two minutes to put their Bible verse strips together.
- Signal when to begin and when to stop. See which teams put the Bible verse strips in the correct order. Let the teams check their strips against the verse you have written on newsprint or let them use their Bibles.
- Give each student a photocopy of today's Bible verse *(Activity Sheet 9)* to decorate and add to her or his journal.

Spiritual Workout

- Ask the students to choose one of the characters in the story of the prodigal son and write about him in their journals.
- Suggest they think of ways that the two brothers could become whole again.

Experiencing God's Shalom

SAY: *Today one of our Key Words is* shalom. *Shalom is God's perfect peace. God wants us to live in peace.*

- Give each student a photocopy of the shalom puzzle *(Activity Sheet 10)*.
- Invite everyone to enjoy the puzzle. Go over the answers: *Shalom, peace, health, wholeness, salvation,* and *justice.* Suggest they add the puzzle to their journals.

Grow and Go

Ask for prayer requests. Write them on a sheet of newsprint. Then pray, thanking God for the class, for stories in the Bible that help us grow, and for God's love in Jesus. Give thanks that no one is beyond God's love. Pray for each prayer request.

- Give each student a photocopy of the prayer *(Activity Sheet 11)*.
- Ask everyone to read the prayer with you to close the session.

Love, Forgiveness, and Healing

Main Idea

Love and forgiveness are important parts of healing.

Scripture

Love each other, as I have loved you. John 15:12, CEV

Key Words

Agape • divine selfless love

Reconciliation • the act of making things right or balanced

Get Ready

- Gather all the supplies you will need for this session.

- Mark 2 Kings 5:1-19 and Matthew 18:21-35 in your Bible.

- Write the Key Words on a sheet of newsprint.

- Write today's Bible memory verse (John 15:12) on a sheet of newsprint.

- Cover the tables with newspapers for the oiled picture activity.

- On another sheet of newsprint list these statements about forgiveness:

  Forgiveness is a gift of grace.

  Forgiveness is always the right thing to do.

  Forgiveness is an act of will.

  The goal of forgiveness is to make relationships right (reconciliation).

  Forgiveness transforms anger.

BIBLE BACKGROUND

John 15:12
2 Kings 5:1-19
Matthew 18:21-35
Luke 15:11-24
Matthew 6:9-13
Luke 11:2-4

SUPPLIES

CEV Bibles
student journals (see p. 6)
photocopies of Activity Sheets 12-18
(pp. 46-52)
3-hole paper punch
newsprint or large pieces of paper
markers, pens, pencils
permanent markers or crayons
small bowls
vegetable oil
cotton balls
newspapers

Welcome

- Welcome the students warmly.

- Ask the students to copy the Key Words for this session and their definitions in their journals. Ask if anyone has heard the words used and what the circumstances were when they heard them.

- Ask the students to copy the statements about forgiveness and put them in their journals.

SAY: *Today we are going to explore how love and forgiveness are important parts of healing—healing for ourselves and healing for others.*

The Power of Love

SAY: *Today we are going to hear the story of Naaman's healing. This story is like no other in the Bible. In it you will discover a compelling and surprising story about the power of love. Naaman's healing is set into motion by a compassionate young Jewish girl, a slave in Naaman's home. Her faith and spirituality suggest that love has tremendous power to release God's healing. Although the word* **love** *is never used in the story, it is strongly implied and its power is evident.*

- Open your Bible to 2 Kings 5:1-19.

- Ask for volunteers to read the verses aloud for everyone to hear. *(If your students do not enjoy reading aloud, read or tell the story to the children.)*

- Give each student a copy of *Activity Sheet 12.*

SAY: *Write one of the three possible responses in the blank by each statement: A for agree, D for disagree, or N for not sure. Do this activity individually. Then share your responses with two other persons.*

- Bring the students back together and go over their answers.

SAY: *This story tells us that everyone can help bring healing to hurting people. It also tells us that we don't have to be perfect or know everything about God for God to heal us. If you love people, God can bring wholeness to others through you. This girl was probably no older than many of you. She shows us what can happen when you reach out to others in love and compassion. It is obvious that the parents of this girl had taught her the Hebrew Scriptures that told her to love both God and her neighbor and to show care to strangers.*

CONTINUE: *She also demonstrates the power of forgiveness. She chose love over anger or revenge. She looked beyond her own needs and saw a greater need in her captor. She chose to show love toward the person who had done her wrong.*

ASK: *What do you think you would have done in her circumstances? (Allow discussion. Let the children be honest.)*

SAY: *The next time you think someone has hurt you, try to respond to him or her in an attitude of forgiveness. Ask God for the grace to express compassion and love to those who wrong you. God may choose to use you, like this girl, as God's healing instrument. Perhaps you too may have an opportunity to turn a person's life around and help him or her experience God's healing grace.*

CONTINUE: *God's vision for us is to make us all whole in the four dimensions of life. They are spirit, body, mind, and relationships. When we focus only on physical healing we often miss God's best and highest good for our lives.*

Make Oiled Pictures

- Give each student a photocopy of the picture of Naaman dipping himself in the Jordan (*Activity Sheet 13*).

- Invite everyone to color the picture using crayons or permanent markers.

SAY: *Forgiveness can be compared to WD-40 Oil. WD-40 Oil is a lubricant for reducing the friction between moving parts made of metal. It makes it easier to loosen metals that have become pressed or tightened together, like a nut and bolt.*

CONTINUE: *Forgiveness is the "spiritual oil" which works in the same way. Forgiveness reduces the friction and eases the hurt feelings between people who have wronged one another. Forgiveness releases God's love. This "spiritual oil" not only reduces the pain of hurt feelings but also releases God's power to bring healing to relationships and help make us whole people. Forgiveness makes reconciliation possible. Reconciliation is the act of making things right or balanced.*

- Cover the work surface with sheets of old newspaper.

- Pour a little vegetable oil into some shallow bowls and give each child a cotton ball.

- When they have finished coloring their pictures, have them dip the cotton balls in the oil in order to apply the oil to their pictures.

- While they are doing this, point out the words about forgiveness on the newsprint.

ASK: *Can anyone tell us the meaning of grace?* (Grace is the love and mercy of God toward us. We do not earn it or deserve it. It is freely given to us.)

SAY: *Forgiving others and even ourselves is hard and challenging work. Knowing this, God gives us a powerful spiritual "hurt buster," "pain remover," and "relationship saver" we call grace. The more we practice forgiveness, the more we live the way Jesus taught us to live.*

Forgive or Not?

- Ask volunteers to read Matthew 18:21-35.

ASK: *How often are we to forgive?* (as often as needed)

SAY: *When Jesus taught about forgiveness, he stressed these points: forgiveness is always the right thing to do; we are to forgive as often as needed; forgiveness transforms evil into good; forgiveness is never a good thing to put off; living in right relationships is everyone's responsibility; broken relationships affect the quality of our worship; and forgiveness and reconciliation are a source of blessedness (goodness).*

- Give each student a photocopy of *Activity Sheet 14*.

- Encourage the students to work together on the activity.

SAY: *We choose to forgive or not forgive. Jesus taught that forgiveness should be offered to everyone, without hesitation—to friends and enemies alike. Remember that he taught that we do not have to deserve God's grace to receive it. Jesus also warned against holding anger inside ourselves. Anger left to simmer in the heart and mind becomes a block to grace. It puts a wall between individuals.*

CONTINUE: *Jesus put all of his teachings on forgiveness into practice, even in his dying moments on the cross. Jesus asked his Father to forgive those who had nailed*

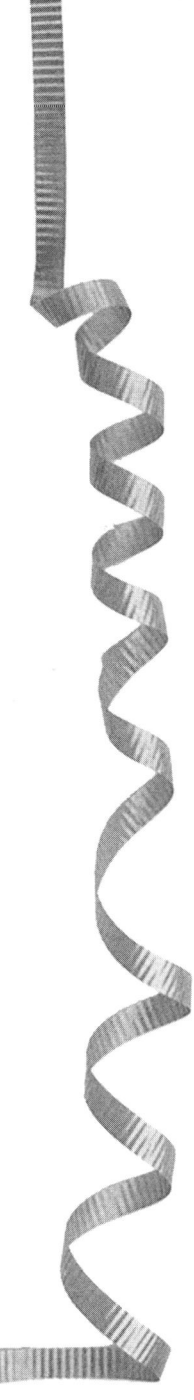

19

him to the cross. He also offered forgiveness to the repentant thief who was being crucified alongside him. Jesus taught us to forgive others in the same way that God forgives us. God's forgiveness is always available to us. Forgiveness is an expression of God's agape love.

Review

- Give each student *Activity Sheet 15.*

- Encourage the students to complete the activity without help. Go over the answers (see p. 64). Make sure they put the puzzle into their journals.

- Recall last week's story of the prodigal son.

- Invite the students to work individually on *Activity Sheet 16.* Assure them that they can keep their answers to themselves if they wish.

Write God's Word on Your Heart

- Point out the memory verse you have written on newsprint.

- Ask everyone to say the verse with you.

- Teach the students how to say the verse using American Sign Language.

Love—Cross your hands at the wrists and press them over your heart.

Each Other (One Another)—Make fists with both hands, with the thumbs out. Hold the right fist with the thumb down. Hold the left fist with the thumb up. Circle the thumbs counterclockwise around each other.

I—Hold up the little finger, with the other fingers curled down. Place the hand at the chest.

You—Point out with your index finger.

- When everyone is comfortable with the signing, ask them to take turns signing to one another.

- Give each student a photocopy of today's Bible verse *(Activity Sheet 17)* to decorate and add to her or his journal.

Spiritual Workout

SAY: *All of us have done something that has hurt someone. But we can be forgiven. In your journal write a letter to God. In the letter ask God to help you go to a person you have hurt and ask for forgiveness. Use this letter to get in touch with your true feelings and to identify any guilt or hurts. Explore and also express your feelings fully to God. Ask God not only to forgive you for the wrong but also to heal the hurt you may have caused the other person. This represents a "trial run" to prepare you personally to ask forgiveness of the person you have wronged.*

Suggested Books

Christmas Moccasins by Ray Buckley (Abingdon Press, 2003) is an excellent, true story of a grandmother modeling and teaching the love and forgiveness of Jesus to her grandson. If you do not have time to read it in class, suggest that the students take turns taking the book home to read and share with their families.

Close With Prayer

SAY: *The Lord's Prayer is found in Matthew 6:9-13 and Luke 11:2-4. The Lord's Prayer is the prayer Jesus taught his disciples to help them know how to pray. We can use the Lord's Prayer as our model to help us better understand God and prayer and to help us know how to express our needs to God. The prayer teaches us about our relationship with God, the Creator; with Jesus Christ, our Savior; with the Holy Spirit; and with one another.*

- Give each student a copy of the prayer *(Activity Sheet 18)*.

- Invite everyone to pray the Lord's Prayer together.

- Encourage the children to put the prayer in their journals.

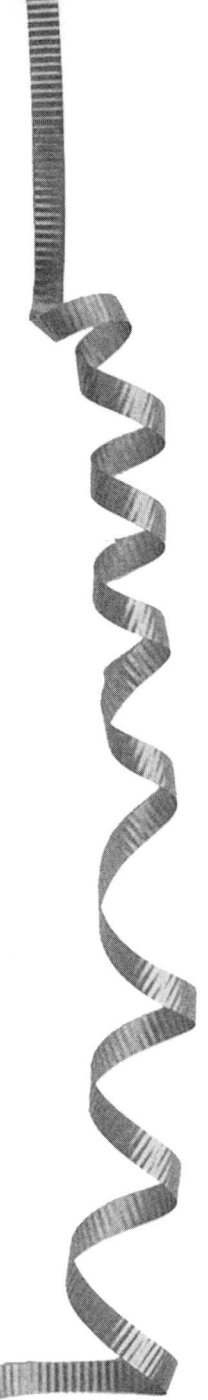

The Four Ways of Healing

Main Idea

Healing can happen in one of four ways.

Scripture

I pray that all goes well for you. I hope that you are as strong in body, as I know you are in spirit. 3 John 1:2, CEV

Key Words

Coping • learning to live with a problem or illness

Healing Miracle • a healing process performed by God that occurs instantly

Get Ready

- Gather all the supplies you will need for this session.
- Mark 3 John 1:2 and Luke 13:10-17 in your Bible.
- Write the Key Words on a sheet of newsprint.
- Write today's Bible memory verse (3 John 1:2) on a sheet of newsprint.
- Remove the labels from soup or vegetable cans and clean the cans.
- In each corner of the room post a sign displaying one of these terms: *miracle, coping, gradual, eternal life.*

Welcome

- Greet the students warmly as they arrive.
- Ask them to copy today's Key Words into their journals.
- Review the Bible memory verses from the earlier sessions.

BIBLE BACKGROUND

3 John 1:2

Luke 13:10-17

SUPPLIES

CEV Bibles

student journals (see p. 6)

photocopies of Activity Sheets 19-22 (pp. 53-5[

3-hole paper punch

newsprint or large pieces of paper

markers, pens, pencils

clean, empty soup or vegetable cans that have the labels removed

scissors

tape

flat-head nails

hammers

small tealight candles

tray of healthy snacks: cheese, crackers, sliced fruit, and napkins

Option: brushes and paint

SAY: *Today we are going to explore four ways of healing. We know that God desires for us to have healthy and whole lives in our bodies, in our minds, in our spiritual lives, and in our relationships.*

Four Ways of Healing—Miracles

• Invite a volunteer to read Luke 13:10-17.

SAY: *Healing can happen in one of four ways. When healing occurs instantly, we call it a miracle.*

ASK: *What is a miracle? Who can perform a miracle? (It is something only God can do.) How was Jesus able to perform a miracle? (Jesus is the Son of God. God gave Jesus the power to perform the miracle.)*

SAY: *A miracle cannot be explained, it just happens. It is a God thing. The bent-over woman was healed instantly. She had given up all hope, but Jesus made her well again and she immediately began praising God.*

Four Ways of Healing—Gradually

SAY: *Most people do not get well in an instant. For most people healing is a gradual process. People may experience healing after much prayer or special medical intervention or help.*

• Ask if someone knows anyone who was sick or injured for a long time but slowly recovered.

Good or Bad Habits?

SAY: *Sometimes a germ or a virus may cause us to be sick and it may take medicine to help us get better. But sometimes healing occurs because we help ourselves. When Mom reminds us to wash our hands before we eat, she is wanting us to stay healthy. It doesn't take long to wash our hands, but sometimes we just ignore our better sense. Not a good idea! We all know that giving up junk food is a good idea, but sometimes we ignore that advice too. Staying up late, fighting with our families and friends, and on and on, these are things that make us unwell.*

SAY: *We have talked about some things that we can do to have a healthy lifestyle. Some of the things we named were eating healthy food, drinking plenty of water, getting enough sleep, exercising, reading books, listening to music, reading the Bible, praying, and helping others. We also talked about things that can keep us from being whole, healthy persons. Some of the things we named were eating unhealthy foods, drinking, smoking, taking drugs, lying, cheating, having bad attitudes, and being unkind to others.*

SAY: *Much of what we do is out of habit. Some habits are good. Some are not. To change a habit, there are some things we must do. First, think about the habit you want to change. What excuse do you have for not changing or that makes changing hard to do? For instance, I do not exercise enough because I am too busy with other things. Next, what are the benefits you will have if you change your habit? For instance, if I were to exercise routinely, I would feel better, have more energy, and look better in the new clothes I just bought. The third thing I should ask is, Who can help me? Is there someone who would like to exercise with me?*

• Give each student a copy of the calendar form *(Activity Sheet 19)* to add to their journals.

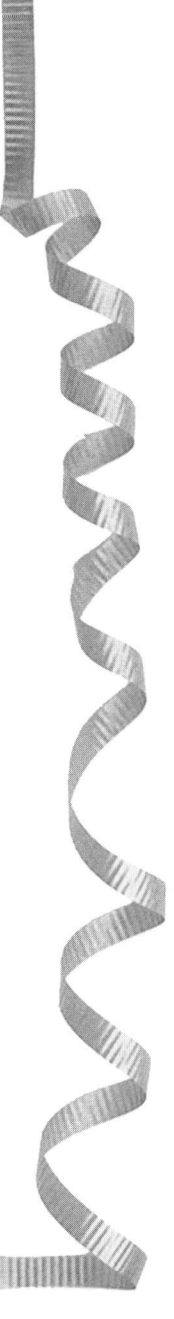

SAY: *Keep a daily calendar for the next thirty days. For each day write one thing you can do to help yourself have a healthy lifestyle. Don't forget to pray for God's help. If you make a slip, just begin again and ask God to help you.*

- Give the students time to work on their calendars. Encourage them to ask one another for help or suggestions.

- When everyone is finished, invite everyone to say a brief, silent prayer asking for God's help.

Four Ways of Healing—Coping

SAY: *A third way of healing is coping. People who use a cane for balance or who wear eyeglasses are coping. People who take medicine to control their blood sugar or their high blood pressure are coping.*

ASK: *Does God love people who are coping as much as God loves people who are healed immediately?* (Yes.)

SAY: *Just because they are not healed does not mean that God does not love them. God created us with brains to use to help all of humankind. New medical procedures are being discovered every day. In the meantime, doctors have found ways to make our lives more whole.*

Four Ways of Healing—Eternal Life

SAY: *In 2000 many people listened as a twelve-year-old boy, Nkosi Johnson, spoke to the International AIDS Conference in Durban, South Africa. Nkosi told an interviewer that he didn't want to die, but he was not afraid of dying. Nkosi appreciated life and did all he could do to live a quality life by taking his medicines three times a day. After a while the medicines stopped working. He stopped taking the medicines and went on with life. Although he realized that he would die, Nkosi worked hard to spread the word that people with AIDS should be treated with dignity and respect. He left us with this challenge: "Do all you can with what you have in the time you have in the place you are."*

- Ask the students to write this statement in their journals and briefly write what it might mean in their lives. Ask if anyone wants to share a journal entry.

SAY: *Sometimes we are not healed until we die. Our bodies were not meant to last forever. In the end, everyone who trusts in Jesus Christ for their salvation will be completely healed. We do not know why healing comes in this life for some and not for others, but we know that in the life to come all sickness, disease, and death will be destroyed.*

- Give each student a copy of the activity "Healing Is . . ." (*Activity Sheet 20*) to complete and add to their journals.

Four Corners Game

- Point out the signs in the corners of the room: *miracle, coping, gradual, eternal life.*

- Ask one student to be IT and sit in the middle of the room. Either wearing a blindfold or with hands over eyes, IT should shout "Get Well!" Have the students scatter to the four corners. When everyone is in place, have IT guess where he or she thinks the most players are. The players in that corner are out of the game.

- Repeat the game with the remaining players. Each time have IT continue guessing until there is one player left. That player becomes the new IT.

Can-Do Cans

SAY: *God sent the Holy Spirit to empower the church with spiritual gifts to help people experience as much health and wholeness as possible. The role of the church is to help people choose lifestyles that bring about healing and wholeness. We are the church and we can help and encourage others to live as healthily as possible.*

ASK: *Is there someone who needs your help or your encouragement to live a healthier lifestyle? Is there someone who needs to hear you say, "You can do this"?*

- Give each student an empty, clean soup or vegetable can that has the label removed.
- Give each student a copy of the patterns *(Activity Sheet 21)*.

SAY: *Select the pattern you want to use. Cut around the pattern and tape the pattern onto the side of your can.*

- Show the students how to use a nail and hammer carefully to punch the pattern into the can.
- Give each student a small tealight candle to put in his or her can.
- Invite each student to write a note of encouragement to place in the can-do can.

Option: Let the students paint the cans or decorate them with permanent markers.

Write God's Word on Your Heart

- Have a tray of healthy snacks: cheese, crackers, sliced fruit, and napkins.
- Ask everyone to read today's Bible verse together two times: "I pray that all goes well for you. I hope that you are as strong in body, as I know you are in spirit" (3 John 1:2, CEV).
- Give one student the tray of snacks to serve to another student while saying today's verse. Have the student who has been served take the tray and serve someone else while saying today's verse.
- Continue until each student has received a snack and has said the verse.
- Give each student a photocopy of the Bible verse *(Activity Sheet 22)* to add to her or his journal.

Spiritual Workout

SAY: *Make an effort to learn how to listen to the messages your body sends to you. If you are tired and grouchy, your body is probably telling you to get more rest and to eat more healthy foods. Ask an adult how he or she learned to listen to the messages that a car sends to a driver. Ask that adult to share his or her secrets. Next, think about how you can respond to the messages your body gives you.*

Close With Prayer

- Invite everyone to pray the Lord's Prayer with you. If any students are still learning the prayer, encourage them to read the prayer from their journals.

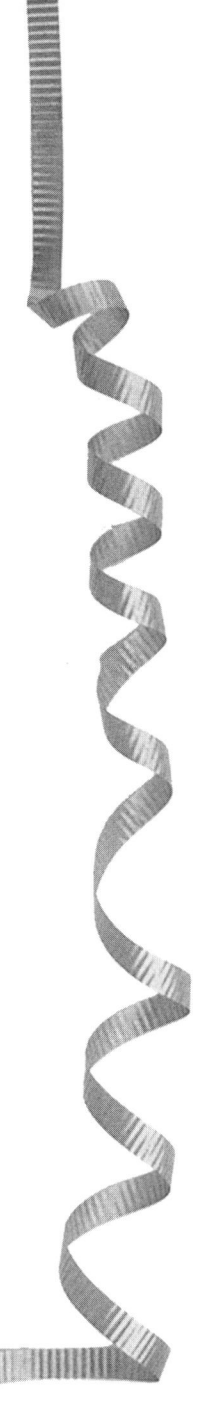

Wholeness of Body, Mind, and Spirit

Main Idea

True well-being happens when we are healthy in our spirit, body, mind (emotions) and relationships.

Scripture

Those who trust the LORD will find new strength. They will be strong like eagles soaring upward on wings; they will walk and run without getting tired.
Isaiah 40:31, CEV

Key Words

Boundaries • limits; lines or things that show us where to stop

Image of God • the ability to act, think, and feel in some of the ways God does

Get Ready

- Gather all the supplies you will need for this session.
- Mark 1 Corinthians 6:19, Genesis 1–2, and James 5:13-15 in your Bible.
- Write the Key Words on a sheet of newsprint.
- Write today's Bible verse (Isaiah 40:31) on a sheet of newsprint.
- Create a "baseball bat" by opening a coat hanger into the shape of a diamond. Cover the diamond with a piece of net or stretch pantyhose over it. Twist down the sharp ends and tape closed.

BIBLE BACKGROUND
Isaiah 40:31
Genesis 1–2
1 Corinthians 6:19
James 5:13-15

SUPPLIES
CEV Bibles
student journals (see p. 6)
photocopies of Activity Sheets 23-24 (pp. 57-58)
3-hole paper punch
markers, pens, pencils
coat hanger
piece of net or pantyhose
duct tape
soft indoor ball
items for cards: cardstock or paper, stickers and other items (lace, paper doilies, scrapbooking items, and so on) to glue to the cards, glue or gluesticks, and envelopes
large sheets of paper

- Label four pieces of paper to be the bases and home plate. On first base write the word *Body*, on second base write *Mind*, on third base write *Relationships*, and on home plate write *Spirit*.

Welcome
- Greet the students warmly as they arrive.
- Ask them to copy today's Key Words into their journals.
- Briefly review the vocabulary words from the previous lessons.

ASK: *Have you ever just felt out of sorts? (Allow discussion.)*

SAY: *Maybe you were getting sick or maybe you were sad or lonely. People of all ages have these feelings. If we are "down in the dumps," we can feel better if someone gives us a hug or a loving smile. If we are overly tired, we can sometimes feel better by getting the rest we need or by changing from eating a lot of junk food to eating healthier foods. Maybe you feel bad because you have lost someone you loved. Friends and family members move away, people we have known and loved die. If you are feeling down because of these things, God has provided people to help you. Talk to your parents, a trusted older neighbor, or your Sunday school teacher or pastor. We are all part of God's great family and God wants us to help each other.*

Plan a Card Shower
- Talk with the students about people in your church who are sick or need encouragement.
- Have cardstock or paper, crayons and markers, stickers and other items *(such as lace, paper doilies, and scrapbooking items)* that can be glued to the card, glue or gluesticks, and envelopes to mail the cards.

SAY: *Each of you can design a get-well card for one of the people named. Make it simple but personal and unique. The main thing is to express compassion, encouragement, and best wishes. Write your favorite Bible verse on the card. We can shower the people receiving your cards with love and care.*

- Explain that you will be responsible for mailing the cards.

Our Bodies Are . . .
- Divide the students into teams of three or four.
- Ask each team to draw the outline of a person's body on a large sheet of paper. If time permits, let the teams enjoy adding hair, eyes, and so forth.

SAY: *Write on the outline of the body the things a person needs to be healthy. (Give the students time to talk and write.) Now write the things a person needs to be happy. (Give the students time to talk and write.) Now write on the outline the things God wants for each of us.*

- Ask each team to tell what they have written on the outlines.
- Allow time for each team to add new thoughts to their outlines as they hear from the other teams.

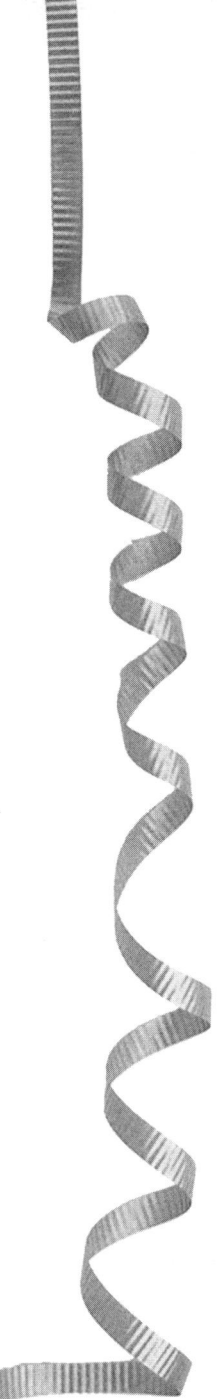

Temple of God

• Ask a volunteer to read 1 Corinthians 6:19.

SAY: *First Corinthians 6:19 tells us our bodies are God's temple. God created our bodies, and God dwells in them through the Holy Spirit. If our bodies are indeed the temple of God, how should we treat our bodies?* (*Accept answers.*)

CONTINUE: *Through the Bible God gave us a great plan for healthful living. God tells us that we should care for the whole person: we should treat our bodies as the temple of God; we should live at peace with our families and neighbors; we should renew our hearts and minds by reading God's Word* (*the Bible*); *and we should think good thoughts. When we do all those things we say that we are living life in the Spirit of God.*

God Gives Us Boundaries

• Ask volunteers to read Genesis 1:27 and 2:8-9, 15-17.

SAY: *Creation was a miracle and God's marvelous creation continues to be a miracle.* (*Briefly retell the story of creation and the fall.*)

SAY: *God met all the needs of those God created. They lacked nothing and lived in a place of safety. It was an exciting time and all was well.*

ASK: *Do you like to play with puppets and action figures? Can they move about and make decisions on their own? Would you like to be an action figure—only able to move when someone else made you?*

SAY: *When we say that we are made in the image of God, one of the things that comes to mind is that God made us to be able to make decisions for ourselves. But all of us need boundaries in our lives. God's plan is for us to live happily and in safety. But God did not want us to be like puppets or action figures. God wanted us to make choices on our own. When people cross boundaries and make wrong decisions, they hurt themselves and others. God set many boundaries for creation— boundaries separating the day from the night, separating the earth, sea, and sky, separating animals that fly in the air from those that live on the earth.*

CONTINUE: *These boundaries were God's way of protecting and caring for the whole of creation. God told Adam and Eve that the tree of the knowledge of good and evil was out of bounds. This seems reasonable, doesn't it—they had the whole rest of the garden! But Adam and Eve did not like the boundary God had set for them. The fruit of that tree looked better than all the other trees to them! Before long they had stepped outside the boundary God had set for them. Inside the boundaries they had lacked nothing. Outside of them they must have felt they were on their own. They had opened the door to lies, deceit, mistrust, and other things that were not a part of God's good creation.*

ASK: *What are some boundaries we have in our lives?*

• Write each suggestion on newsprint. With each boundary, ask, "Is this boundary good for us? Why or why not?"

SAY: *When we live inside the boundaries God has set for us, we can live as whole, healthy persons in body, mind, and spirit.*

Life Is Like a Baseball Game

- Plan this activity in a large, open area.

- Set out the "bat" and bases you prepared earlier. Have a soft indoor ball to play with.

- Divide the group into two teams. Decide who will be the pitcher for each team.

- Invite the teams to play baseball for a few minutes.

SAY: *Consider the analogy of the game of baseball to better understand how to enjoy more health and wholeness in your life. What is the object of baseball?* (*to hit the baseball and to run the four bases to make a score*) *Think of the game of life or health as being like the game of baseball.*

CONTINUE: *Each batter stands at home plate to take his or her turn to hit the baseball. Every batter hopes at least to get on the base by hitting the ball without being thrown out by the defensive team. Of course, the batter wants to run all four bases to score a run or point. Life is like a baseball game. In order to experience well-being, you must work the four dimensions of life. When you work to enhance your health in all four areas of life, you will experience more wholeness. When you make this a lifestyle, you will have a greater level of health in every level or stage of life. We are to exercise good stewardship for our bodies.*

ASK: *Whether you are playing baseball or the game of life, does it make sense to strive to get only to first base?* (*No.*)

SAY: *However, most people today still think only about their physical health. They care only for their bodies, and disregard their spiritual, mental, and relational health. They are satisfied with getting only on first base. If you want to have the best possible health, you must run the four bases each day. If a baseball team only hit the ball to get to first base, and not to cross home plate, the team would win few or no games. The game would not be exciting to watch. The same is true with our health. The goal of well-being is to the win the game of life. Part of experiencing the abundant life is to work for wholeness in the four dimensions of life. To neglect one is to neglect the others. Let's get in the game of life and run all of the bases to enhance our well-being.*

Write God's Word on Your Heart

- Point out the newsprint with today's verse and ask everyone to say it with you.

SAY: *Eagles can be as much as 40 inches long and weigh 10 pounds or more. They have a wingspan of 6 to 8 feet. They have a lifespan of up to 30 years in the wild, and longer in captivity. They can fly to altitudes of 10,000 feet or more, and can soar aloft for hours using natural wind currents. Isaiah was using the analogy of the eagle to help the people know that God would give them strength.*

- Give each student a copy of today's Bible verse (*Activity Sheet 23*).

- Invite the students to color the picture and add it to their journals.

SAY: *Healing is a mystery. We do not know why some people are healed and others are not. Only God knows how, when, and to whom healing might occur. Healing does not always happen the way we might expect it to happen. What we do know is that healing is possible and it does happen often. The fact that Jesus spent considerable*

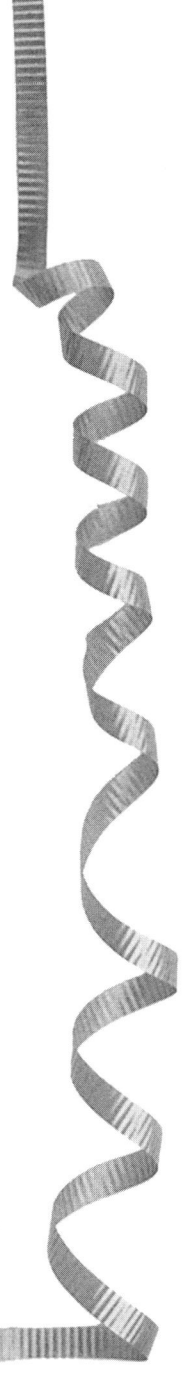

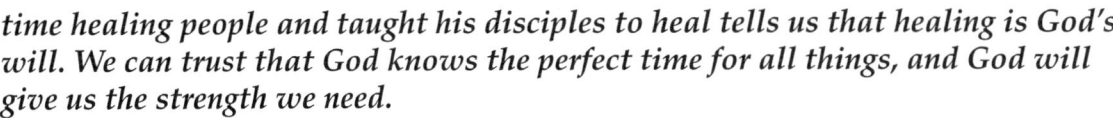

time healing people and taught his disciples to heal tells us that healing is God's will. We can trust that God knows the perfect time for all things, and God will give us the strength we need.

Suggested Book

Have a copy of *The Wing* by Ray Buckley. Read the book together and point out that the bird was healed in an unexpected way. Encourage the students to take turns enjoying the book at home with their families.

Spiritual Workout

- Ask volunteers to read James 5:13-15.

- Give each student a copy of "People I Want to Pray For" *(Activity Sheet 24)*.

SAY: *Put this in your journal. Follow the directions. When you pray for the people you list, pray from your heart. God will hear your prayers.*

Close With Prayer

- Lead the students in an open-ended prayer. Let each student have an opportunity to add his or her own ending.

PRAY: *Dear God, thank you for your healing love. We trust you to give us strength. We ask . . .*

Healing in Eternity

Main Idea
Jesus gives us new, everlasting life.

Scripture
Jesus then said, "I am the one who raises the dead to life! Everyone who has faith in me will live, even if they die. And everyone who lives because of faith in me will never really die." John 11:25-26, CEV

Key Word
Metamorphosis • change or transformation in the development of an animal

Get Ready
- Gather all the supplies you will need for this session.
- Mark 1 Corinthians 15:35-58 in your Bible.
- Write the Key Word on a sheet of newsprint.
- Write today's Bible verse (John 11:25-26) on a sheet of newsprint.
- Write these phrases on a sheet of newsprint:
  What Jesus has done for me
  What Jesus has done for someone I know
  Something I am thankful for
  Something I like about this group

Note to Leaders
This final lesson is about death. Some of your students may have had the experience of losing someone close to them. All of them may know someone from church who has died. If they have questions you can't answer, don't hesitate to say that you don't know. Explain that there are some things that will remain a mystery to us until we get to heaven. Remind the students that sometimes healing does not come until we do get to heaven.

Welcome
- Greet the students warmly as they arrive. Tell them how much you have enjoyed watching them grow in their understanding of health and wholeness during the past weeks.

- Ask the students to copy today's Bible memory verse and dictionary word into their journals.

BIBLE BACKGROUND
John 11:25-26
1 Corinthians 15:35-58
Psalm 23

SUPPLIES
CEV Bibles
student journals (see p. 6)
photocopies of Activity Sheets 25-29 (pp. 59-63)
3-hole paper punch
markers, pens, pencils, crayons
newsprint or large sheets of paper
brown construction paper
scissors
stapler and staples
glue
bowl of candy

ASK: *Have you ever had someone you love die?* (Accept answers.) *What was the hardest part for you?* (Accept answers.)

SAY: *Today we will discover that when someone dies, that person lives on in our memories and in heaven. Jesus gives new, everlasting life.*

Eternal Life

• Read 1 Corinthians 15:35-58 to the students or ask several volunteers to read portions of the verses.

SAY: *God expects us to take care of the wonderful bodies God gave us. God wants us to live long and fulfilling lives. It is true that we can do many things to harm these thoughtfully and wonderfully made bodies. But when we do that, it is something we bring on ourselves, not something God sends.*

ASK: *What are some things we do that harm our bodies?* (poor eating habits, poor habits of sleep and recreation, taking drugs or drinking alcohol)

SAY: *Taking good care of our bodies will help them last longer, even if we are born with a chronic illness* (an illness that is always present and does not go away). *But eventually everyone does die. Even after Jesus came back from the dead he did not stay on earth forever, but went to heaven to be with his Father and all those who love and obey God.*

SAY: *Life is a beautiful thing. As we observe the metamorphosis* (change) *of a butterfly, we also discover that the new life we have with Christ after death is also a beautiful thing.* **Metamorphosis** *simply means change. The New Testament tells us that death is a transition, a change, to more life—eternal life. In death we are changed (transformed) into the likeness of Jesus Christ.*

Create a Chrysalis

• Give each student a copy of *Activity Sheet 25*.

• Have crayons, brown construction paper, and scissors ready for everyone to use.

• Have the students cut out all the pieces, but color only the body of the butterfly (*not the wings*) at this point.

• Have them use the chrysalis or cocoon shape as a pattern to cut two shapes from the brown construction paper.

• Lay the activity aside.

SAY: *Both life and death are mysteries. However, God has this whole issue of life and death figured out for us. God uses both for God's divine purposes. We don't understand death, so we fear it. And we love life so we hate to leave it. Even Jesus prayed that somehow God might change things so that he would not have to die. God wants us to live and enjoy life. But God does not want us to take our lives for granted.*

CONTINUE: *For many of us, it takes a lifetime to discover why we have been put on this earth. As we grow older we may be reminded that we have spent too much time putting things off. We should live every day fully, in peace with our families and friends. Time here on earth is a gift that we need to use wisely. When we accept that life is a gift, each new day becomes an adventure. When we embrace the notion that life is to be lived to its fullest and that life is to be shared with others, nothing can shake our faith—not even death.*

CONTINUE: *Jesus taught and encouraged his followers to live their lives by sharing the time they have with others.*

- Return to the butterfly activity and have the students color the rest of the pieces.

As they work, **SAY:** *The butterfly can only develop when it has gone through all the stages of metamorphosis. The fuzzy caterpillar spins a cocoon in which it rests and develops. When all the changes have taken place it is transformed into a beautiful butterfly.*

- Let them place one cocoon shape on top of the other and staple the two pieces together, leaving an opening at the top for the butterfly.

- Have them color the words "Jesus Gives New Life" and glue this square onto the brown chrysalis.

- Ask everyone to write today's Bible memory verse on the blank side of the butterfly, then fold the butterfly in half with the colored side on the inside. Then fold each wing backward down to the center fold. Part of each colored wing is now on the outside.

- Let the students place the butterfly inside the cocoon.

SAY: *When the butterfly emerges from the cocoon it has been transformed. We could think of the opening it makes in the cocoon as a doorway to new life. Without going through the door of death, we cannot receive our new bodies.*

CONTINUE: *Our new bodies will be indestructible. People who have been ill all their lives here on earth will be healed and will never be sick again. This new life came as the result of Jesus' death and resurrection. If we trust in God's Son for our salvation, there is no fear in death, because God's love for us is perfect, and perfect love removes all fear.*

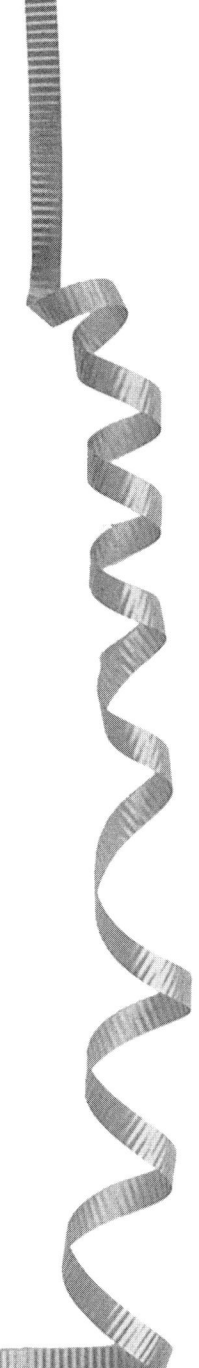

Words of Comfort and Encouragement

- Ask each student to select a partner.
- Give each student a photocopy of *Activity Sheet 26*.
- Let the partners work together to complete the activity. Give them any help they may need.
- Let them put the activity sheet in their journals.

Psalm 23

SAY: *King David wrote a psalm that gave him courage as he lived and gave him hope for the future after death.*

- Invite a volunteer to read Psalm 23 from a CEV Bible.

ASK: *What words in this psalm take away your worry or fear?*

- Give each student a photocopy of *Activity Sheet 27*.

SAY: *Unscramble the words on the activity sheet. Then complete the sheet and add it to your journal.*

- Go over the answers with the students (see p. 64).

Write God's Word on Your Heart

- Display the newsprint with today's memory verse. Ask everyone to say the verse with you several times.
- Give each student a copy of the crossword puzzle (*Activity Sheet 28*).

SAY: *The answers to this puzzle are in today's verse.*

- Allow time for the children to work through this puzzle.
- Go over the answers with the students (see p. 64).
- Give each student a copy of today's verse (*Activity Sheet 29*) to add to her or his journal.
- Review the memory verses from all the sessions. Encourage the students to try to say the verses without looking at their journals or the newsprint, but tell them it is perfectly all right to read the verses if they cannot remember them.
- Encourage them to keep their journals and read the verses often.

Suggested Book

Have on hand a copy of *We Are All the Same: A Story of a Boy's Courage and a Mother's Love* by Jim Wooten (Penguin Press, 2005). Encourage the students to take turns enjoying the book at home with their families.

Spiritual Workout

SAY: *Jesus gives new, everlasting life. Each of us can have a personal relationship with Jesus. Let's think about our lives and our experiences.*

- Have everyone sit in a circle.
- Pass a bowl of candies around the circle. Tell the students that they may each have as many as four pieces of candy.
- Point out the newsprint with the four phrases on it.

SAY: *Count the number of candies you have. For each piece of candy, respond to one of the phrases. If you have fewer than four candies, you may pick which phrases to respond to.*

Close With Prayer

- Ask for any prayer concerns the students might have and list them on newsprint.
- Pray for each one. Then pray for each child by name, thanking God for his or her life. Praise God for being with us when we are sick and when we are well. Ask for God's help in living the life God wants us to live.

Nametags

Word Search

Use your detective skills to learn about God's special creation. Find these hidden words and circle each one. Don't forget to look across, up, down, diagonally, and backwards! These words are all found in Psalm 139:13-16.

BODY	EYES	ONE
BOOK	EVERYTHING	PRAISE
BORN	HIDDEN	SECRETLY
CREATED	INSIDE	TOGETHER
DEEP	MARVELOUS	WONDERFUL
EARTH	NOTHING	WOVEN

```
E  A  R  T  H  X  X  X  B  O  R  N  Q  X
V  X  X  X  X  Y  X  X  X  X  X  X  X  D
E  X  S  U  O  L  E  V  R  A  M  X  V  E
R  V  X  X  X  X  Q  X  X  X  X  Q  X  T
Y  V  X  X  Q  Y  X  B  O  O  K  X  V  A
T  X  Q  Q  T  X  Q  X  X  X  X  X  X  E
H  H  Q  Q  N  O  T  H  I  N  G  X  X  R
I  I  X  X  V  X  G  X  X  X  S  Q  Q  C
N  D  X  X  Q  Y  X  E  X  Q  E  X  X  X
G  D  N  Q  E  X  Q  Q  T  X  C  X  X  Q
X  E  E  X  D  V  X  A  X  H  R  X  Q  X
P  N  V  X  I  V  Q  X  Q  X  E  Y  E  S
P  V  O  X  S  X  D  X  X  X  T  R  X  X
P  V  W  O  N  D  E  R  F  U  L  X  X  Q
X  X  X  X  I  V  E  Q  X  Q  Y  X  Q  X
X  E  S  I  A  R  P  V  Q  X  X  X  X  Q
O  N  E  X  Q  X  X  X  Q  B  O  D  Y  X
```

Jeff Steinberg

Since I was born with no arms and two badly bent legs, you might not think that I am "fearfully and wonderfully made." Often when my wife and I go out, people act shocked to see a short man whose one artificial arm has a hook attached to it. They cannot get past my appearance to see me. But I have come to realize that it is not my outward form that makes me wonderful.

My parents were unable to care for me, but my heavenly Father was always directing and guiding me as I was moved from place to place. At the Shriners Hospital, I was fitted for my first arm and had many surgeries that enabled me to walk. Just down the street from Good Shepherd Home, my last group home, was a storefront Mennonite church whose Sunday school teachers came week after week to take me and other children to church. They made me a part of their lives and loved me. Together with one of my nurses, they taught me that I, Jeff Steinberg—born with no arms and twisted legs—am fearfully and wonderfully made.

Since the day I asked the Lord Jesus to come into my life, what others call "handicaps" have become a springboard for me to share God's love with a lost and dying world.

Prayer
O God, help us to see your loving hand at work in our lives and to know that each of us can be used in your service. Amen.

Thought for the Day
   Each of us is fearfully and wonderfully made.

Jeff Steinberg

Originally published in *The Upper Room Magazine*, January–February 2006 issue, copyright 2005 by The Upper Room, PO Box 340004, Nashville, TN 37203-0004. This material is used by permission of Jeff Steinberg and The Upper Room, Inc.

True or False?

Which of the statements do you agree or disagree with?
Answer T (True) or F (False) by each statement.

___ Jesus found this man disgusting because he was a leper.

___ This miracle teaches us about who Jesus was.

___ Jesus healed the leper both by his touch and by his words.

___ A person with leprosy was considered an untouchable (unclean).

___ It was forbidden for a leper to have physical contact with uninfected people.

___ The leper fully believed that Jesus had the power to heal him.

___ Lepers were allowed to travel about freely.

___ Because Jesus loved this man, he touched him, even if it meant he would become "unclean" also.

___ Jesus encouraged his disciples to heal lepers as he had done.

___ The healing of the leper did more than heal his body. Jesus also restored him to his family, community, and synagogue.

TO CHECK YOUR ANSWERS read Luke 5:12-16.

I praise you because of the wonderful way you created me. Everything you do is marvelous!

Psalm 139:14, CEV

Word Power!

Use each of these words in a sentence that will explain what you will do to take care of your body and have a healthy lifestyle.

Food or Diet_____

_____

Exercise_____

_____

Rest_____

_____

Attitude_____

_____

Love_____

_____

Forgiveness_____

_____

Smoking_____

_____

Drugs/Alcohol_____

_____

fold

I am thinking of u

Bible Verse Strips

Real love isn't our love for God, but his love for us. God sent his Son to be the sacrifice by which our sins are forgiven. Dear friends, since God loved us this much, we must love each other.

1 John 4:10-11, CEV

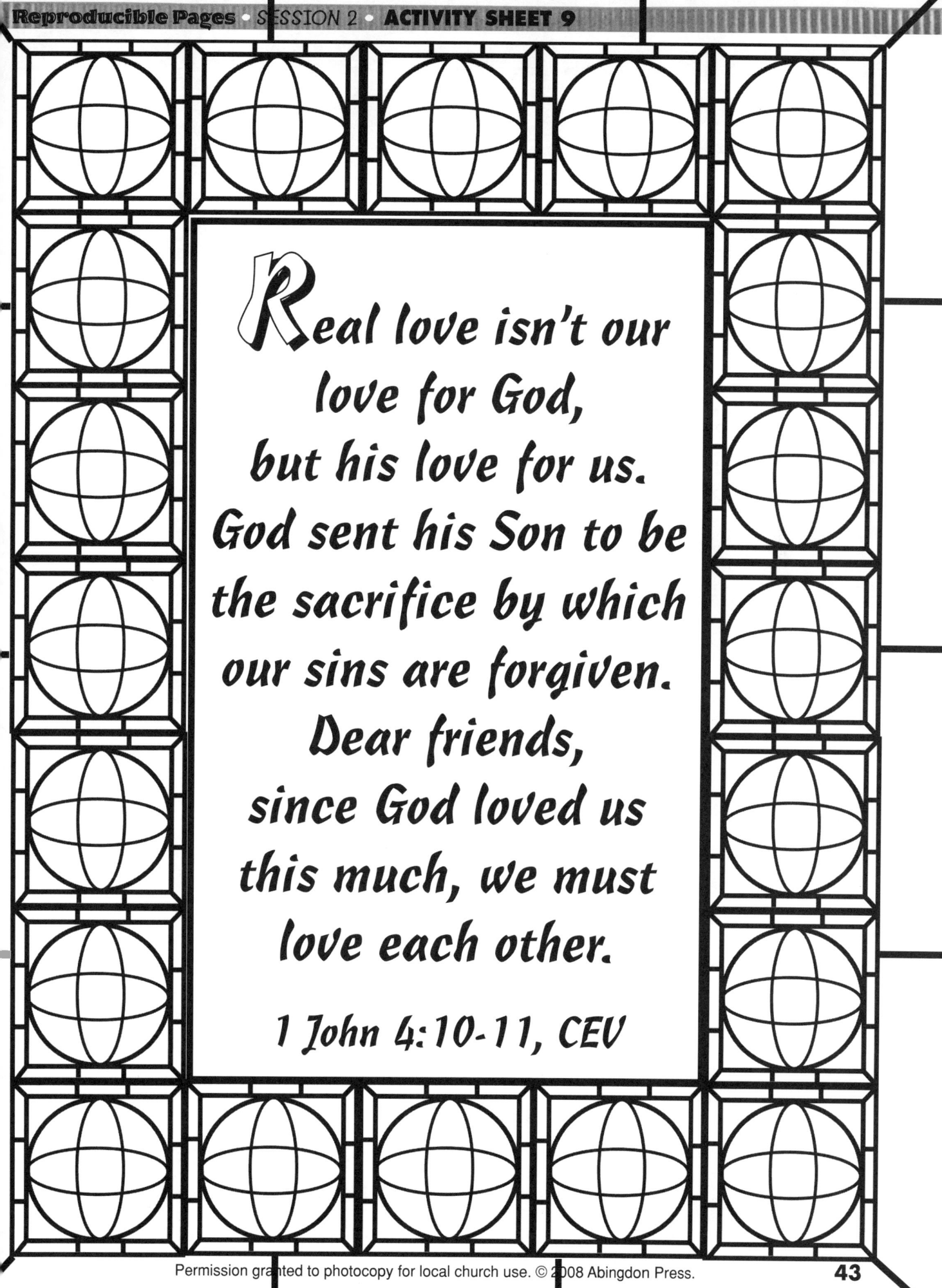

Real love isn't our
love for God,
but his love for us.
God sent his Son to be
the sacrifice by which
our sins are forgiven.
Dear friends,
since God loved us
this much, we must
love each other.

1 John 4:10-11, CEV

Experiencing God's Shalom

Unscramble each of the following words and use the words to complete the sentences.

1. mlhoas
2. eecap
3. laehht
4. hesnewols
5. vitaslano
6. citesuj

1. _ _ _ A _ _ _ _

2. _ _ _ _ C _

3. _ E _ _ _ _ H

4. _ _ _ _ L _ _ E _ _ _

5. _ _ L _ _ _ _ _ N

6. J _ _ _ _ _ C _

S_ _ _ _ _ _ means more than p_ _ _ _. It is a word that describes the fullness of the abundant life that God desires for us.

Shalom means h_ _ _ _ _ _, w_ _ _ _ _ _ _ _ _ _ _, peace, s_ _ _ _ _ _ _ _ _ _, j_ _ _ _ _ _ _, and blessedness that can only be fully experienced through a personal relationship with God.

Creator God,

Thank you for how wonderfully and thoughtfully you created me.

Forgive me for not accepting the way you made me.

I know that I am special, because you created me out of your love and grace.

You not only created me out of love, you created me for yourself—for your divine purpose.

I have been wrong to think of myself in negative ways.

I now know that I was in your heart and mind before the world was formed.

I am a work in process. You are not done with me yet.

Help me to accept who I am and whose I am—your child!

Amen.

Agree or Disagree?

Read the statements below.
Write **A** if you agree, **D** if you disagree, and **N** if you are not sure.

___ God wants to heal everyone, including people who do not yet know God.

___ Only perfect people can be healed.

___ God's healing power is available to everyone who wants to be made whole.

___ Every person can be healed.

___ The young Jewish girl did not resent her captor. Instead she showed him love and forgiveness.

___ Healing is rooted in love.

___ Everyone can help others to heal.

ANGER

Answer **T** (true) or **F** (false) by each statement.
Your teacher may have to help you with some of the answers.

___ Insulting a person is just as harmful and hurtful as hitting that person with your fist.

___ Insulting a person's name or ethnicity is acceptable behavior.

___ Forgiveness is an action of love.

___ Forgiveness is necessary to keep your relationships healthy and growing.

___ No one is required to love an enemy.

___ Broken relationships affect the quality of your worship of God.

___ Regardless of whose fault a conflict is, you should make the first move toward making it right.

___ Jesus taught that every wrong done to another person should be taken seriously.

___ You need to forgive a person only seven times.

___ A person should lie to keep from getting into more trouble.

___ Not forgiving others has no effect on how God might forgive you.

___ The Lord's Prayer suggests that forgiveness should be a daily concern.

___ Forgiveness is supposed to be a part of our lifestyle.

Forgiveness is Transforming

Forgiveness brings together human needs with God's healing power. When you forgive, you are working with God to bring healing in a hurting world. See if you can complete the statements below by using the code to fill in the missing words.

Forgiveness is transforming because:

A	B	C	D	E	F	G	H	I
1	2	3	4	5	6	7	8	9

J	K	L	M	N	O	P	Q	R
10	11	12	13	14	15	16	17	18

S	T	U	V	W	X	Y	Z
19	20	21	22	23	24	25	26

1. It transforms __ __ __ __ __.
       1 14 7 5 18

2. It provides you with __ __ __ __ __.
       7 18 1 3 5

3. It reveals the __ __ __ __ __ __ __ of God.
       11 9 14 7 4 15 13

4. It makes __ __ __ __ __ __ __ __ __ __ __ __ __
     18 5 3 15 14 3 9 12 9 1 20 9 15 14
possible.

5. It liberates the __ __ __ __ __ __ __ person into
       9 14 10 21 18 5 4
God's healing stream of grace.

6. It enables you to fulfill the Great Commandments: to __ __ __ __ God with all your heart, soul, mind, and
   12 15 22 5
strength, and your neighbor as yourself.

7. It allows you to choose a __ __ __ __ __ __ __ __ __ __
       14 15 14 22 9 15 12 5 14 20
path toward others.

8. Forgiveness is always the __ __ __ __ __ thing to do.
       18 9 7 8 20

Forgiveness Is an Act of the Will

The decisions you make in life have either good or bad results. You can see this played out in the story of the prodigal son in Luke 15:11-24. Read those verses and complete the activity below.

1. What choices did the prodigal son make that got him into trouble and also created a conflict in his relationship with his father?

2. What choices did he make that got him out of trouble and restored his relationship with his father?

Bad Choices
Good Choices

3. Name a wrong choice you have made that led you into some conflict with your father or another family member. What steps will you take to put right that relationship?

Love each other, as I have loved you.

John 15:12, CEV

The Lord's Prayer

**Our Father,
who art in heaven,
hallowed be thy name.
Thy kingdom come,
thy will be done
on earth as it is in heaven.
Give us this day our daily bread.
And forgive us our trespasses,
as we forgive those who
trespass against us.
And lead us not into temptation,
but deliver us from evil.
For thine is the kingdom,
and the power,
and the glory,
forever.
Amen.**

Calendar

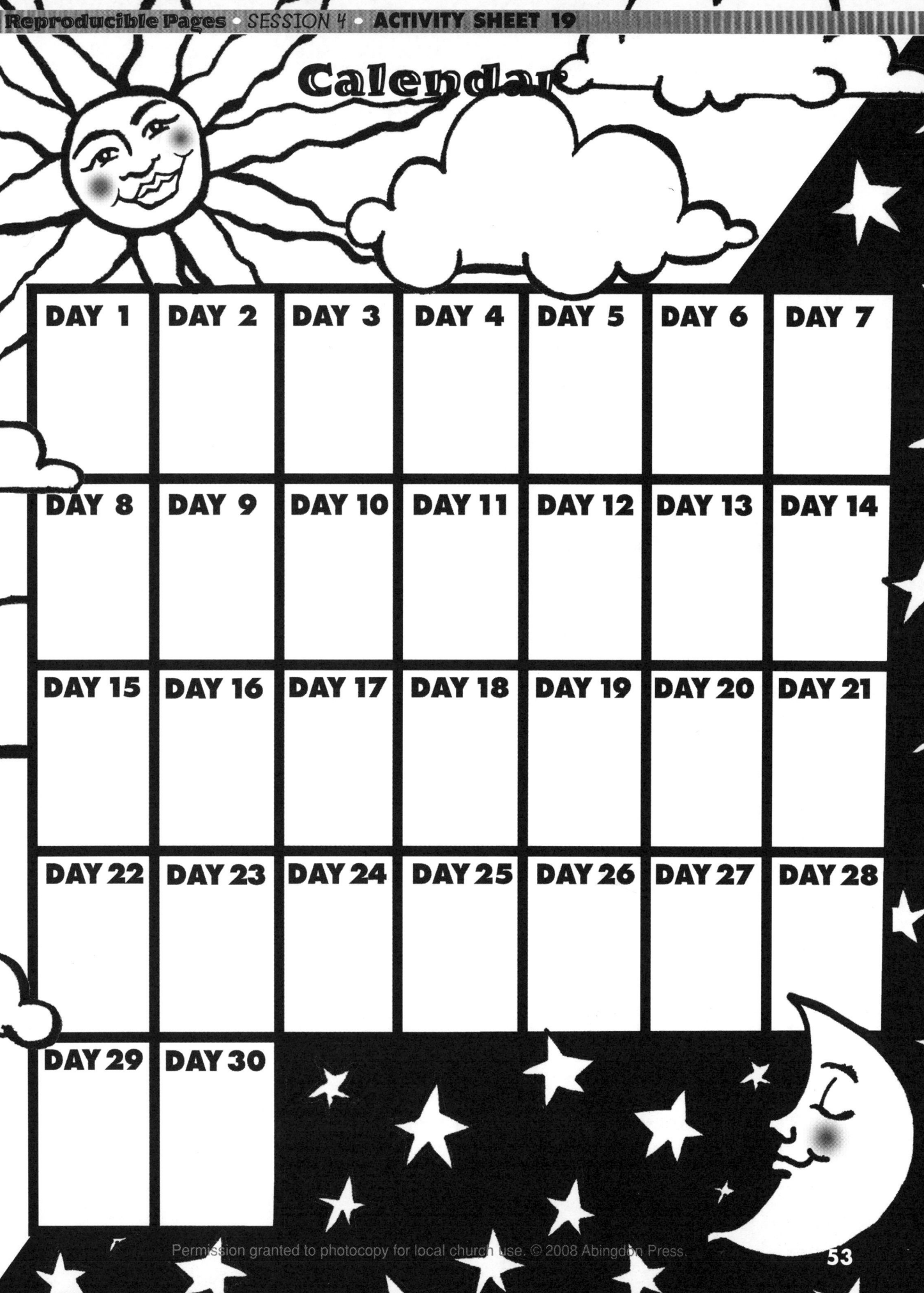

DAY 1	DAY 2	DAY 3	DAY 4	DAY 5	DAY 6	DAY 7
DAY 8	DAY 9	DAY 10	DAY 11	DAY 12	DAY 13	DAY 14
DAY 15	DAY 16	DAY 17	DAY 18	DAY 19	DAY 20	DAY 21
DAY 22	DAY 23	DAY 24	DAY 25	DAY 26	DAY 27	DAY 28
DAY 29	DAY 30					

Healing Is...

Complete the statements to describe your understanding of healing.

1. Healing reminds me that _____.

2. Healing may not always occur _____.

3. Whether healing happens or not, I still know _____
_____.

4. It is God's desire _____.

5. God heals both sinners and _____.

6. God heals through _____.

7. God loves me and wants _____.

8. God can heal us even if our faith is as small _____
_____.

9. Healing can occur _____.

10. My prayer is that God will heal _____.

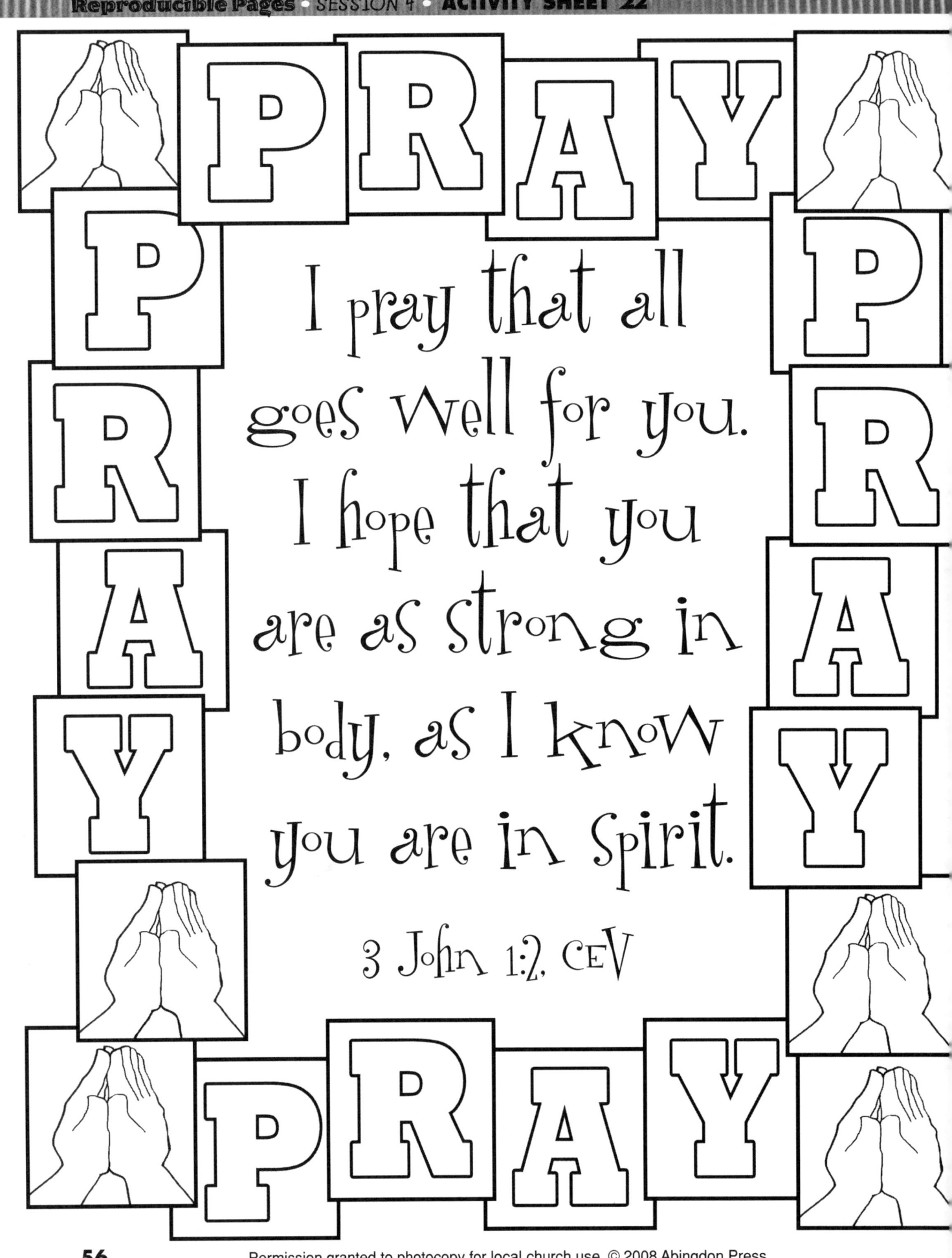

I pray that all goes well for you. I hope that you are as strong in body, as I know you are in Spirit.

3 John 1:2, CEV

Those who trust the LORD will find new strength. They will be strong like eagles soaring upward on wings; they will walk and run without getting tired.

Isaiah 40:31, CEV

People I Want to Pray For

The apostle James teaches us to pray at all times and pray for one another. When you pray for a sick person, you release God's healing power for that person and for yourself. That is the power of agape love (God's love). When you release God's love, it continues to flow and those nearby also get blessed. If you start a fire to warm a cold friend, you also are warmed by the fire. Your prayers for others set God's love on fire to heal.

Think of four people who need healing. Plan to pray for each person for one week. Write their names below. You may list a friend, a family member, a church member, or a neighbor. When you pray, use your imagination to see each person you are praying for (including when you pray for yourself) surrounded by God's love and healing power.

Week 1_____

Week 2_____

Week 3_____

Week 4_____

Focus your healing prayer on God's love. Remember that healing is rooted in agape love. Your prayers release God's healing love and power for the good of others and yourself.

Words of Comfort and Encouragement

The Bible gives us glimpses into the transition or change that takes place in the resurrection. Look up these passages and write in the space a word or an idea that helps you better understand the meaning of resurrection and the power of the cross.

1 Corinthians 15:35-37 _____

1 Corinthians 15:38-39 _____

1 Corinthians 15:42 _____

1 Corinthians 15:43-44 _____

1 Corinthians 15:50-54 _____

1 Corinthians 15:55-57 _____

David's Words

In Psalm 23, David used certain key words which gave him courage, confidence, and assurance that he would not face death alone. See how many of those words you can find. Unscramble the words on this page and meditate on their meanings.

1. ssendkni
2. feas
3. fceelapu
4. ters
5. frhsere

_ _ _ D _ _ _ _ _

_ _ _ E

_ _ A _ _ _ _ _

_ _ _ T

_ _ _ _ _ _ _ H

Which of these words has the deepest meaning for you as you think about death?

_____

Give each word a value from 1 to 5, with 1 as the highest value and 5 as the lowest value.

1 _____

2 _____

3 _____

4 _____

5 _____

Team Up!

1. **2.**

4.

3.

Jesus said,
"I am the one
who raises the dead
to life! Everyone
who has faith in
me will live, even
if they die. And
everyone who lives
because of faith in me
will never really die."
—John 11:25-26, CEV

7.

5.

6.

To solve this puzzle, decide what each picture shows and write the first
letter of that word in the proper blank below. For example, the first box
shows a jacket, so the letter J belongs in the first blank after the number 1.

1. __ __ __ __ __ • 2. __ __ __ __ __ __ __

3. __ __ __ __ __ __ • 4. __ __ __ __

5. __ __ __ __ • 6. __ __ __ • 7. __ __ __

Jesus then said, "I am the one who raises the dead to life! Everyone who has faith in me will live, even if they die. And everyone who lives because of faith in me will never really die."

John 11:25-26, CEV

Answers

Activity Sheet 2, page 36, Word Search

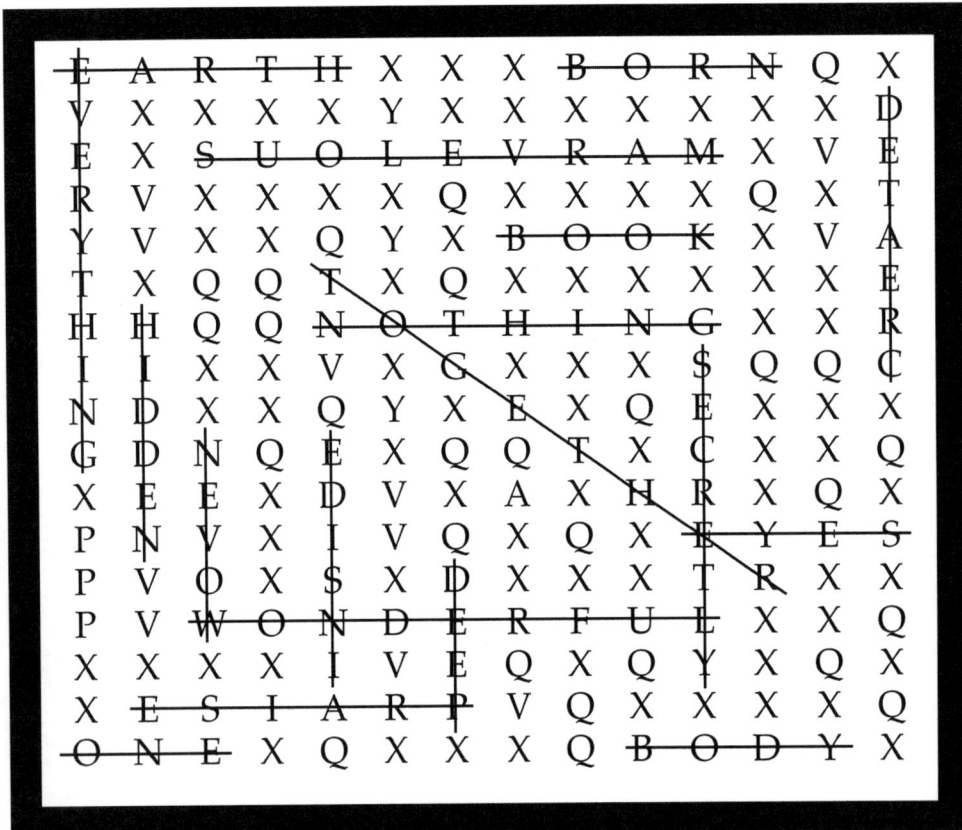

```
E A R T H X X X B O R N Q X
V X X X X Y X X X X X X X D
E X S U O L E V R A M X V E
R V X X X X Q X X X X Q X T
Y V X X Q Y X B O O K X X A
T X Q Q T X Q X X X X X X E
H H Q Q N O T H I N G X X R
I I X X V X G X X X S Q Q C
N D X X Q Y X E X Q E X X X
G D N Q E X Q Q T X C X X Q
X E E X D V X A X H R X Q X
P N V X I V Q X Q X E E Y E S
P V O X S X D X X X T R X X
P V W O N D E R F U L X X Q
X X X X I V E Q X Q Y X Q X
X E S I A R P V Q X X X X Q
O N E X Q X X X Q B O D Y X
```

Activity Sheet 10, page 44, Experiencing God's Shalom
1. shalom
2. peace
3. health
4. wholeness
5. salvation
6. justice

Activity Sheet 27, page 61, David's Words
1. kindness
2. safe
3. peaceful
4. rest
5. refresh

Activity Sheet 15, page 49, Forgiveness Is Transforming
1. anger
2. grace
3. kingdom
4. reconciliation
5. injured
6. love
7. nonviolent
8. right

Activity Sheet 28, page 62, Team Up!
1. Jesus *(jacket, eye, sun, umbrella, snowman)*
2. everyone *(eye, vacuum cleaner, ear, rat, yacht, octopus, nest, egg)*
3. raises *(robot, apple, ice cream, snail, ear, squirrel)*
4. faith *(fish, apple, igloo, ten, hat)*
5. never *(nest, elephant, violin, eel, rhinoceros)*
6. one *(ostrich, net, egg)*
7. dead *(donkey, eel, angel, dog)*